The Message of
THE CROSS

*For the message of the cross is foolishness
to those who are perishing, but to us who are
being saved it is the power of God.*

I Corinthians 1:18

Christian Family Church and World Outreach Center
2300 Heritage Place NW | Owatonna, MN 55060
info@cfcchurches.org | www.cfcchurches.org

Legacy Books

Table of Contents

Introduction

This book may very well be the most important book you ever read. If you are not familiar with the message contained herein, it is definitely the most important information you will ever encounter in your lifetime.

Nearly everyone has some familiarity with the symbol of *the cross*. The cross is visible nearly everywhere we go. It is displayed in artwork, people wear it as jewelry around their necks, in their ears, on broaches, tattoos, and, of course, the cross is commonly displayed on church buildings, steeples and in church sanctuaries.

When displayed, the cross sends a message. Yet, some may *think* they know what the message of the cross is but have not actually heard the biblical truth of its real meaning.

Don't underestimate the value of what you are about to read. The message contained within these pages has powerfully touched and changed millions of lives over the past 2000 years, not to mention their eternal destinies. It may very well do the same for you.

Be blessed,
Dr. Tim Peterson

Chapter 1

Perishing or Being Saved?

For the message of the cross is foolishness to **those who are perishing, but to us who are being saved** it is the power of God.

I Corinthians 1:18

The apostle Paul, in writing to the church at Corinth, tells us that there are two kinds of people:

> **#1 = Those who are perishing**
> **#2 = Those who are being saved**

Those who are *perishing* believe that the message of the cross is foolishness. The Passion Translation says, *"To preach the message of the cross seems like sheer nonsense to those who are on their way to destruction."* (I Corinthians 1:18) However, those who are being *saved* believe that the message of the cross is the power of God for salvation.

Everyone is either *perishing or being saved*. So, what exactly does it mean *to be perishing*? What does it mean *to be saved*? And what do either of these have to do with the cross of Jesus Christ?

The word *perishing* means *to suffer death*. In other words, those who do not believe the message of the cross will *suffer death*. But doesn't everyone eventually experience death? Of course they do, if we are talking only about physical death. However, the death which the apostle Paul is speaking of is **eternal death**. Those who do not believe the message of the cross will suffer eternal death. (More detail about eternal death will be covered in Chapter 2.)

The word *saved* or *salvation* means *to deliver from the power of sin and its consequences*. In other words, those who believe the message of the cross will be delivered from sin and its consequences including eternal death which is the ultimate consequence of sin. Those who believe the message of the cross will be saved from eternal death and given the gift of eternal life. Jesus said it like this:

> "For God so loved the world that He gave His only begotten Son that **whoever believes in Him should not perish but have everlasting life.**"

> John 3:16

Why will those who don't believe the message of the cross perish? Why must someone believe the message of the cross to be saved from perishing? Why must someone believe the message of the cross to receive the gift of eternal life?

Chapter 2

The Wages of Sin

For the wages of sin is death, but the gift of God is eternal life in Christ Jesus our Lord.

Romans 6:23

In order to understand why those who do not believe the message of the cross must perish and why those who do will be saved, one must understand the origin of sin and its consequences.

In the book of Genesis we read about God creating the heavens and the earth and everything in it including humankind. When He created the first human beings, Adam and Eve, He placed them in the Garden of Eden to cultivate and protect it. At the same time He gave them instructions as to what they could and could not do, kind of like what any parent would do.

> [15] Then the Lord God took the man and put him in the garden of Eden to tend and keep it. [16] And the Lord God commanded the man, saying, "Of every tree of the garden you may freely eat; [17] **but of the tree of the knowledge of good and evil you shall not eat, for in the day that you eat of it you shall surely die."**

Genesis 2:15-17

God not only *commanded* Adam and Eve not to eat from the tree in the middle of the garden, but also told them what the consequences would be if they did. He clearly articulated to them that the consequences of their disobedience to His command would result in death. The Hebrew literally states, "in dying you will surely die." In other words, they would die a plurality of deaths. Their sin would cause a plethora of consequences including both physical and eventually eternal death, the ultimate consequences of sin.

In the apostle Paul's epistle to the Romans we read:

When Adam sinned, the entire world was affected. Sin entered human experience, and death was the result. And so death followed this sin, casting its shadow over all humanity, because all have sinned.

Romans 5:12
The Passion Translation

Adam opened the door for death, both physical and eternal death, to come into the earth. The scriptures go on to say, **"because of [*this*] one transgression, we are all facing a death sentence with a verdict of 'Guilty!'"** (Romans 5:16b, The Passion Translation)

The Apostle Paul goes on to say:

[17a] **Death once held us in its grip, and by the blunder of one man [Adam], death reigned as king over humanity.** [19b] So also one man's [Jesus'] obedience opened the door for many to be made perfectly right with God and acceptable to him.

Romans 5:17a, 19b
The Passion Translation

Although created to live forever, humankind became mortal and without God's gift of eternal life they would eventually die both physically and eternally.

Chapter 3

The Gift of God

For the wages of sin is death, but **the gift of God is eternal life** in Christ Jesus our Lord.

Romans 6:23

Although Adam and Eve's sin brought a curse upon all of humankind – ultimately resulting in physical and eternal death – God had a plan for humankind's salvation. This gift of salvation, namely eternal life, would be offered to all who believed. This free gift is being offered to all through the cross of Jesus Christ the Lord.

What did Jesus Christ do to provide humankind with a means of salvation from the consequences of original and personal sin? *This is what is called the gospel – the message of the cross.* Jesus Christ, the God-man, took our sins upon himself while on the cross, so we could be forgiven and pardoned from our sentences of physical and eternal death.

God designed a plan of salvation for all humankind through Jesus Christ before the foundations of the earth (Revelation 13:8; I Peter 1:20). God's plan was for His son to bear the sins of the world and take the ultimate penalty of sin – physical and eternal death – upon Himself *in our place.* He became our *substitute* so we could be saved from physical and eternal death.

The prophet Isaiah spoke of God's plan of salvation through the Messiah hundreds of years before the plan was set in motion in real time. Isaiah prophesied:

[4] **Surely he has borne our griefs and carried our sorrows; yet we esteemed him stricken, smitten by God, and afflicted.** [5] **But he was wounded for our transgressions, he was bruised for our iniquities; the chastisement for our peace was upon him**, and by His stripes we are healed. [6] All we like sheep have gone astray; we have turned, every one, to his own way; **and the Lord has laid on Him the iniquity of us all.** [7] He was oppressed and He was afflicted, Yet He opened not His mouth; He was led as a lamb to the slaughter, and as a sheep before its shearers is silent, So He opened not His mouth. [10] **Yet it pleased the Lord to bruise him; He has put him to grief. when you make his soul an offering for sin, he shall see his seed, he shall prolong his days, and the pleasure of the Lord shall prosper in his hand.** [11] He shall see the labor of His soul, and be satisfied. **By his knowledge My righteous Servant shall justify many, for he shall bear their iniquities.** [12] Therefore I will divide him a portion with the great, and he shall divide the spoil with the strong, **because he poured out his soul unto death, and he was numbered with the transgressors, and he bore the sin of many, and made intercession for the transgressors.**

Isaiah 53:4-7, 10-12

Isaiah prophetically told us that God would lay upon the Christ the iniquity (sin) of us all. Through this coming Savior, sin and its consequences would be dealt with once and for all for all humankind.

The New Testament writers tell us the same concerning God's plan of salvation. In the gospel of John we read:

> The next day John saw Jesus coming toward him, and said, **"Behold! The Lamb of God who takes away the sin of the world!"**

John 1:29

The Savior, God manifest in flesh, arrived in the person of Jesus Christ of Nazareth. He came to remove our sins and its consequences and offer the gift of eternal life to all who choose to believe the message of the cross.

The apostle Peter speaking of God's plan of salvation said:

> [18] **knowing that you were not redeemed with corruptible things, like silver or gold,** from your aimless conduct received by tradition from your fathers, [19] **but with the precious blood of Christ, as of a lamb without blemish and without spot.** [20] He indeed was foreordained before the foundation of the world, but was manifest in these last times for you [21] who through Him believe in God, who raised Him from the dead and gave Him glory, so that your faith and hope are in God.

I Peter 1:18-21

Peter tells us that we are saved through the precious blood of Christ, God's perfect lamb, without spot or blemish. The apostle Paul said:

**And, having made peace through the blood
of the cross, by him [Jesus]** to reconcile all
things to himself; by him, I say whether they
be things in the earth, or things in heaven.

Colossians 1:20

The precious blood of Christ *which he shed on the
cross* is what bought and paid for our sins and their eternal
consequences, so that God could offer each and everyone of
us the gift of eternal life.

Chapter 4

Why the Cross?

²⁵ Now it was the third hour, and they crucified Him. ²⁶And the inscription of His accusation was written above: THE KING OF THE JEWS. ²⁷ With Him they also crucified two robbers, one on His right and the other on His left. ²⁸ So the Scripture was fulfilled which says, "and He was numbered with the transgressors." ²⁹ **And those who passed by blasphemed him, wagging their heads and saying, "Aha! You who destroy the temple and build it in three days, ³⁰ save yourself, and come down from the cross!" ³¹ Likewise the chief priests also, mocking among themselves with the scribes, said, "He saved others; Himself He cannot save.** ³² Let the Christ, the King of Israel, descend now from the cross, that we may see and believe." Even those who were crucified with Him reviled Him.

Mark 15:25-32

What the revilers didn't know was that if He saved himself, He could not save us. His death upon the cross was necessary for our salvation.

What the revilers couldn't see was that this sacrificial Lamb was taking the chastisement of our peace upon himself (Isaiah 53:5).What they could not see was God placing the sins of the world upon His sacrificial Lamb, the Lord Jesus Christ (Isaiah 53:6). What they couldn't see was the Lamb of God being offered up in our place (Isaiah 53:10). What they couldn't see was that Jesus was God's Passover Lamb being offered up on the cross for them. They couldn't see nor understand any of these things because they were spiritually blind and hard-hearted towards God. He had told them time and time again that He would come and what He would do when He came.

Why the cross? Because God chose THE CROSS to enact His plan of salvation. *He chose one of the most horrific and gruesome forms of death to show humankind the seriousness and devastation of their sin.*

Sinful humanity was judged by the righteous Judge of heaven to be worthy of death. Our sin was not judged as the equivalent of *a misdemeanor*. Our sin was judged by Almighty God, the Maker of the heavens and the earth, to be equivalent to that of *a capital crime deserving of the death penalty.* God, the all-wise, fair and just Judge of the universe, found humankind worthy of death. This reveals to us the seriousness of our sin and the kind of plan of salvation which was needed to correct it.

Most people and all false religions and cults attempt to make our crime of sin so little and insignificant that humanity could somehow pay their own penalty for their sin as if it were simply a misdemeanor with God. They propose such things as being good, believing in God, church membership, and many other types of man-made inventions to remedy their own sin. However, there is only one remedy for sin and that is the sacrificial death of God's Son on the cross. Only He, the Lord Jesus Christ, could pay our judgement for us. Only He, the perfectly sinless man, could take the penalty for our sin in our place.

The apostle Paul, in his letter to the church at Philippi, explained it like this:

> [6] He [Jesus] existed in the form of God, yet he gave no thought to seizing equality with God as his supreme prize. [7] **Instead he emptied himself of his outward glory by reducing himself to the form of a lowly servant. He became human!** [8] **He humbled himself and became vulnerable, choosing to be revealed as a man and was obedient. He was a perfect example, even in his death—a criminal's death by crucifixion!** [9]Because of that obedience, God exalted him and multiplied his greatness! He has now been given the greatest of all names! [10] The authority of the name of Jesus causes every knee to bow in reverence! Everything and everyone will one day submit to this name—in the heavenly realm, in the earthly realm, and in the demonic realm. [11] And every tongue will proclaim in every language: "Jesus Christ is Lord Yahweh," bringing glory and honor to God, his Father!

Philippians 2:6-11
The Passion Bible

Theologians call this the Kenosis passage. In simplest of terms, it tells us that God came to earth in the person of Jesus Christ. He humbled himself to the point of becoming fully human and died on a cross in our place, to reverse what Adam had set in motion in the Garden of Eden making salvation available to all.

Chapter 5

It Is Finished!

Then Pilate ordered Jesus to be brutally beaten with a whip of leather straps embedded with metal. ² And the soldiers also wove thorn-branches into a crown and set it on his head and placed a purple robe over his shoulders. ³ Then, one by one, they came in front of him to mock him by saying, "Hail, to the king of the Jews!" And one after the other, they repeatedly punched him in the face.

John 19:1-3
The Passion Translation

The preparations for Jesus' crucifixion were not pretty. He was *brutally beaten with a whip of leather straps embedded with metal.* "This leather whip, embedded with sharpened pieces of bone and metal, was known as 'the scorpion'. Historians record that many people never survived this cruel flogging. The whips were known to break open the flesh and cut through muscle and sinew all the way to the bone." [1]

They also placed a *crown of thorn-branches* on his head pressing it deep down to his skull. They dressed him up in purple to mock him for saying that he was a king – the King of the Jews – and repeatedly took turns punching him in the face.

---

1 The Passion Translation, p. 297, see note b

The Crucifixion

[17] Jesus carried his own cross out of the city to the place called "The Skull," which in Aramaic is Golgotha. [18] **And there they nailed him to the cross. He was crucified, along with two others, one on each side with Jesus in the middle.** [19-20] Pilate had them post a sign over the cross, which was written in three languages—Aramaic, Latin, and Greek. Many of the people of Jerusalem read the sign, for he was crucified near the city. The sign stated: "Jesus of Nazareth, the King of the Jews." [21] But the chief priests of the Jews said to Pilate, "You must change the sign! Don't let it say, 'King of the Jews,' but rather—'he claimed to be the King of the Jews!' " [22] Pilate responded, "What I have written will remain!"

John 19:17-22
The Passion Translation

He was nailed in the palms of each hand and in both feet (John 20:25, 27). But it wasn't *these* nails alone which kept Jesus nailed to the cross; *it was our sin and His love for us*.

He hung between two robbers (Matthew 27:39; Mark 15:27), both of which were also hurling insults and ridicules at him (Matthew 27:39; Mark 15:29).

Over Jesus' head Pilate also posted a sign. Every convicted criminal, who was crucified under Roman rule, had a sign placed over their head indicating the kind of crime for which he was being crucified. Over Jesus' head Pilate also posted a sign. Jesus' sign said, "Jesus of Nazareth, King of the Jews." However, the chief priests wanted the sign changed to "He claimed to be the King of the Jews." Pilate refused to make the change.

The sign was written in three languages – Aramaic, Latin, and Greek. "Aramaic was the language of the common people in Israel. Hebrew ceased to be their spoken language after 450 BC, after the Jews returned from Babylon. Aramaic remained the language of Israel for nearly one thousand years. Latin was the official language of the Roman Empire. The inscription was also in Greek, for the Alexandrian Jews who had come to observe the Passover in Jerusalem were unable to read Aramaic. The first letters of each of the first four words written on the sign in Aramaic (Hebrew) were: Y-H-W-H (Y'shua Hanozri Wumelech a Yehudim). To write these letters, YHWH (also known as the Tetragrammation), was the Hebrew form of writing the sacred name "Yahweh." No wonder the chief priests were so offended by this sign and insisted that Pilate change it. This was a sign given to Israel, for over Jesus' head on the cross was written, Y-H-W-H! God, the Savior, bled to death for you." [2]

The four Latin letters of each of the first four words are INRI. The letter "I" represents Jesus' name spelled Iesus. Although Latin has a letter "J" in their alphabet, it was decided to spell Christ's name beginning with an "I", probably because Aramaic and Greek do not have a letter "J" in their alphabets. The letter "N" in INRI stands for Nazarenrs, which in English is Nazareth or Nazarene. The letter "R" stands for Rex, which is translated "King". The last letter "I" is an abbreviation for the word Irdaeonum, which translated is "Jews" (again, using "I" in place of using "J"). In English, the literal meaning or definition is "Jesus Nazareth King Jews." [3] The four Greek letters of each of the first four words are INBI.

Why three languages? Latin was the official language of the Roman Empire, Greek was the international language of the culture, and Aramaic was the religious language of the Jews.

2 The Passion Translation, p. 299, note a
3 ChristianAnswers.net

The Mission Accomplished

28 Jesus knew that his mission was accomplished, and to fulfill the Scripture, Jesus said: "I am thirsty." 29 A jar of sour wine was sitting nearby, so they soaked a sponge with it and put it on the stalk of hyssop and raised it to his lips. 30 **When he had sipped the sour wine, he said, "It is finished, my bride!"** Then he bowed his head and surrendered his spirit to God.

John 19:28-30
The Passion Translation

Jesus, the Christ of God, knew what his mission on earth was and knew when he had fulfilled it. He left his glorious state of Heaven and became a man for the purpose of redeeming humankind. He knew that his mission would end at the Cross. He had fulfilled everything God's plan of salvation had required of him. Therefore, his last words before bowing his head and surrendering his spirit back to God were, "It is finished!" The mission was finished. The demands of justice from the heavenly court system and the Divine Judge Himself were satisfied. **The plan of salvation was accomplished.**

Humankind could now receive a pardon from their crimes (sins) against God. God's eternal judgement was paid for once and for all. Everyone was now qualified to receive God's offer of eternal life.

Which group of people will you choose to be a part of that the apostle Paul talked about in I Corinthians 1:18, mentioned at the beginning of this book? *Will you be one of those who think that the message of the cross is absurd and foolish, or will you join the ranks of those who believe the* *message of the cross is the power of God for salvation and be saved? **It's your choice!***

Chapter 6

It's Your Choice!

The Lord is not slack concerning His promise, as some count slackness, but is longsuffering toward us, **not willing that any should perish but that all should come to repentance.**

II Peter 3:9

The *choice* is yours. You can either join the ranks of *those who are perishing* or *those who are being saved* (I Corinthians 1:18). The truth is, God doesn't want anyone to miss out on His plan of salvation through Jesus Christ on the Cross. He desires for all to COME TO SALVATION: every man, every woman, and every child.

So how does someone receive what Jesus Christ did for them at the Cross? How does one receive God's gift of salvation personally? How can someone know for sure that their sins are forgiven, their sentence of eternal death has been overturned, and that they have received the gift of eternal life?

Here are four biblical steps to help you receive God's gift of eternal life through Jesus Christ's substitutionary work on the Cross and get started on your walk with God:

STEP #1 = BELIEVE

Dear friends, let me give you clearly the heart of the gospel that I've preached to you—the good news that you have heartily received and on which you stand. [2] **For it is through the revelation of the gospel that you are being saved, if you fasten your life firmly to the message** I've taught you, unless you have believed in vain. [3] For I have shared with you what I have received and what is of utmost importance: **The Messiah died for our sins, fulfilling the prophecies of the Scriptures.** [4] **He was buried in a tomb and was raised from the dead after three days, as foretold in the Scriptures.** [5] Then he appeared to Peter the Rock and to the twelve apostles.

I Corinthians 15:1-5
The Passion Translation

Receiving the gift of salvation begins with believing the message of the cross. The message of the cross is Jesus died for our sins, was buried, and rose again from the grave (death) the third day.

This message which the apostles began preaching over 2,000 years ago, and for which they were willing to give their lives, is not foolishness or utter nonsense. It is the eternal truth and power of God for salvation.

The apostle John closed out both his gospel and first epistle with these powerful words about *believing* in God's plan of salvation through Jesus Christ:

But these are written that you may believe that Jesus is the Christ, the Son of God, **and that believing you may have life in His name**.

John 20:31

These things I have written to you who believe in the name of the Son of God, that you may know that you have eternal life, and that you may continue to believe in the name of the Son of God.

I John 5:13

The apostle Paul said the following about the power of believing:

But no one earns God's righteousness. It can only be transferred when we no longer rely on our own works, but believe in the one who powerfully declares the ungodly to be righteous in his eyes. **It is faith that transfers God's righteousness into your account!**

Romans 4:5
The Passion Translation

Our faith in Jesus transfers God's righteousness to us and he now declares us flawless in his eyes. This means we can now enjoy true and lasting peace with God, all because of what our Lord Jesus, the Anointed One, has done for us.

Romans 5:1
The Passion Translation

Other references stating the importance of believing the message of the cross can be found in: John 3:16; Acts 15:7, 16:31; Romans 10:9-14; I Corinthians 1:21; I Thessalonians 2:13, 4:14; II Thessalonians 1:10; I Timothy 1:14, 4:10; Hebrew 10:39, 11:16; I Peter 1:21, 2:7; I John 3:23.

STEP #2 = REPENT

⁴⁶ Then He [Jesus] said to them [the disciples], "Thus it is written, and thus it was necessary for the Christ to suffer and to rise from the dead the third day, ⁴⁷ **and that repentance and remission of sins should be preached in His name to all nations,** beginning at Jerusalem."

Luke 24:46-47

The preaching of repentance has always been and will always be an important part of God's message to humankind. The word *repent* means *to turn away from sin (evil) and turn back to God.*

Jesus, just prior to ascending back to heaven, told his disciples to preach repentance and remission of sins in His name to everyone (Luke 24:46-47). Repentance – turning away from the sins that plague an individual's life and turning toward God in righteousness and holiness – is an important part in receiving God's gift of salvation through Jesus Christ.

The apostle Paul writes about the importance of repentance for salvation in his epistle to the church at Corinth when he said:

⁹ **Now I rejoice, not that you were made sorry, but that your sorrow led to repentance.** For you were made sorry in a godly manner, that you might suffer loss from us in nothing. ¹⁰ **For godly sorrow produces repentance leading to salvation**, not to be regretted; but the sorrow of the world produces death.

II Corinthians 7:9-10

The *sorrow* of which the apostle Paul speaks is the conviction of the Holy Spirit over one's personal sins when they hear the gospel message taught or preached under the inspiration of the Holy Spirit. When an individual feels sorrow and remorse for their personal sin, this sorrow may be one of two types: *worldly sorrow* or *godly sorrow*.

Worldly sorrow simply means that *the transgressor is sorry that they got caught for their act or acts of sin,* whereas godly sorrow *is the conviction that one has sinned against God and needs the forgiveness of a holy God.* Godly sorrow results in one confessing their sins and asking God to forgive them and help them turn away from their life of sin to live a life of holiness pleasing to God.

Are you ready to repent? Are you ready to *turn* away *from your sin* and *turn toward God* and live a holy life pleasing to Him?

This doesn't mean that you will never sin again. But what it does mean is that you will want to please God in all you do and say while depending on the power of the Holy Spirit in your life to do so.

Other references showing the necessity of repentance in a person's life who has believed the message of the cross are: Matthew 3:2-8, 4:17, 9:13; Mark 1:15, 2:17, 6:13; Luke 3:7-8, 5:2, 15:7; Acts 2:38, 3:19, 5:31, 11:18, 17:30, 20:21, 26:20; Romans 2:4; II Timothy 2:25; Hebrews 6:1; Revelation 2:5, 16, 21, 22, 3:3, 19.

STEP #3 = BE BAPTIZED

"He who believes and is baptized will be saved;
but he who does not believe will be condemned."

Mark 16:16

Although much could be said about water baptism, let it suffice to say that Jesus commanded it and made it part of the journey of our Christian life. No writer of the New Testament nor any of the other original apostles would have ever even entertained the notion that someone could call themselves a Christian without obeying Christ's command to be baptized.

Every convert to the Christian faith, as recorded in the book of the Acts of the Apostles, was immediately baptized following their acceptance of the gospel message. (Acts 2:37-38, 41; 8:5, 12; 10:47-48; 16:13-15, 25-34; 18:8; 19:1-5)

Perhaps one of the most significant and graphic, yet seemingly unknown passages of scripture concerning water baptism, is found in Colossians 2:11-12:

> [11] **In Him also you were circumcised with a circumcision not made with hands, but in a [spiritual] circumcision [performed by] Christ by stripping off the body of the flesh (the whole corrupt, carnal nature with its passions and lusts).** [12] **[Thus you were circumcised when] you were buried with Him in [your] baptism,** in which you were also raised with Him [to a new life] through [your] faith in the working of God

[as displayed] when He raised Him up from the dead.

Colossians 2:11-12
Amplified Bible

In water baptism Christ Jesus himself performs a spiritual circumcision of the heart in which He cuts off the guilt and power of sin in our lives. Consequently, water baptism plays a significant role in our relationship to sin no longer having power over us.

The apostle Peter weighs in heavily on water baptism also when he says:

> [18] For Christ also suffered once for sins, the just for the unjust, that He might bring us to God, being put to death in the flesh but made alive by the Spirit, [19] by whom also He went and preached to the spirits in prison, [20] who formerly were disobedient, **when once the Divine longsuffering waited in the days of Noah, while the ark was being prepared, in which a few, that is, eight souls, were saved through water.** [21] **There is also an antitype which now saves us--baptism** (not the removal of the filth of the flesh, but the answer of a good conscience toward God), through the resurrection of Jesus Christ,

I Peter 3:18-21

Peter tells us that the story of Noah is a prophetic picture of how we are saved *through* water. Just like Noah wasn't saved *by* the floodwaters, neither are we saved *by* the waters of baptism. However, just like Noah was saved *through* the floodwaters, we also are saved *through* the waters of baptism.

Noah was saved *through* the floodwaters because of his *obedience* to God. So we too are not saved *by* water baptism, but we are saved *through* the waters of baptism because of our faith in, identification with and obedience to Jesus Christ.

Other powerful passages concerning water baptism are found in: Matthew 3:13-17, 28:18-20; John 3:23, 4:1; Acts 2:37-39, 41; 8:5-8, 12; 10:44-48; 16:13-15, 25-33; 18:8; 19:1-5; 22:12-16; James 2:7 Amplified Bible.

STEP #4 = FIND A GOOD CHURCH

---

[46] So continuing daily with one accord in the temple, and breaking bread from house to house, they ate their food with gladness and simplicity of heart, [47] praising God and having favor with all the people. **And the Lord added to the church daily those who were being saved.**

Acts 2:46-47

God believes in His church and He designed for you and everyone who receives His plan of salvation to become part of a local church. *The church is God's gift to you to help you become a fully devoted and fully committed follower of Christ.*

A good church will believe that the Bible is God's Holy Word. Each week, in this kind of church, you will hear the pastor preaching from the Bible.

A good church will be led by a man of God whom God has called to pastor that particular church. The pastor will be a man of godly character who loves the flock God has placed him over to love, guide, and protect.

A good church will believe in the power and ministry of the Holy Spirit. The supernatural gifts of the Holy Spirit such as miracles, healings, words of knowledge, words of wisdom, tongues, interpretation of tongues and prophecy will be welcomed and evidenced by the church body.

A good church will be an outreach church obeying the Great Commission of Jesus to bring the gospel to others outside of the church both locally and globally.

A good church will be a group of people, however small or big, that love God, love each other and love those who still need Christ. The Lord Jesus put a very high premium on love when he said:

> [34] **"A new commandment I give to you, that you love one another; as I have loved you**, that you also love one another. [35] By this all will know that you are My disciples, if you have love for one another."

John 13:34-35

Do not underestimate the need to find a good church as it is of utmost importance to your spiritual life and journey. Begin attending and do so every week. Make it a habit for you and your family to be in the House of God on the Lord's Day (Sunday) every week. (See my book entitled, "Remember the Lord's Day to Keep it Holy!")

If you are ready to believe in the message of the cross and receive God's gift of salvation, pray the following prayer from your heart.

Lord Jesus,

I know that I am a sinner. I understand that I was judged guilty by the courts of heaven, placing me under a penalty of eternal death, and I cannot save myself.

I want to thank you for coming to earth and dying for me on the Cross in my place. I am sorry for my sins and I ask you to forgive me. I choose to turn away from any and every thing you and the Bible call sin, and learn to love what you love and hate what you hate.

I invite you to come into my life and be my Lord and Savior. I totally and completely commit myself to obeying you for the rest of my life.

Thank you, Jesus. Amen.

Other Books Written by Dr. Tim Peterson

Powerful Faith Producers

The Baptism of the Holy Spirit

Four Steps to Receiving Your Miracle from God

The Law of Sowing and Reaping

The High Cost of Passivity

God Was Manifest in the Flesh

God Incognito – Revelation into the Mystery of God

Beginning at Jerusalem

Prepare for War

A Kingdom of Kings and Priests

Heresy Alert: Justification by Faith Only?

Living in the Paradise of God – Restoration of the Blessing

Taking a Vow of Financial Prosperity for the Sake of the Gospel

The Healing, Miracle, & Deliverance Ministry of Jesus

Walking in Divine Favor

Remember the Lord's Day to Keep It Holy

Receiving the Extravagant Giving Anointing

Living Beneath an Open Heaven

Once Saved, Always Saved. No Way!

The Great Exchange: The Blessing for the Tithe!

Crowned with Glory and Honor!

The History of the Pentecostal Movement

How to Fulfill Your God-Given Dreams!

Understanding Basic Doctrines

Understanding the Gospel Message

Understanding the Local Church

Understanding God the Father, Son, and Holy Spirit

Christian Foundation Series Manual

Driving Out Weakness, Sickness, and Premature Death from Your Body and Life

Made in the USA
San Bernardino, CA
29 February 2020